SCIENCE
in Action
MY SENSES

SMELL

Sally Hewitt

Quarto
Library

This library edition published in 2016
by Quarto Library., an imprint of QEB Publishing, Inc.

6 Orchard, Lake Forest, CA 92630

© 2016 QEB Publishing,
Published by Quarto Library.,
an imprint of Quarto Publishing Group USA Inc.

Distributed in the United States and Canada by
Lerner Publisher Services
241 First Avenue North
Minneapolis, MN 55401 U.S.A.
www.lernerbooks.com

A CIP record for the book is available from the Library of Congress.

ISBN 978 1 60992 882 7

Printed in China

Publisher: Maxime Boucknooghe
Editorial Director: Victoria Garrard
Art Director: Miranda Snow
Series Editor: Claudia Martin
Series Designer: Bruce Marshall
Photographer: Michael Wicks
Consultant: Kristina Routh

Picture credits
t = top, b = bottom, c = center, l = left, r = right,
fc = front cover

Corbis 5 Norbert Schaefer, 6 Bill Stormont, 14b Julie Houck, 15t Tom Stewart, 15b Rick Gayle Studio, 16b Walter Smith, 17t Paul Barton, 18b Ariel Skelley, **Getty Images** 9t Billy Hustace/Photographers Choice, 19 (background) Scott Van Dyke/Beateworks **Shutterstock** fc holbox/AKI's Palette/azure1/ Yoko Design, 6 Cindy Goff, 7t PathDoc, 7b Air Images, 9t Leonard Zhukovsky, 9b kzww, 10b Emena, 14t JPagetRFPhotos, 18t Amanda Hsu, 20t naihei, 20c Nengloveyou, 20b Nengloveyou

Words in **bold** can be found in the glossary on page 22.

Contents

Smell this!

You have five main senses that give you information about the world around you.

The five senses are smell, touch, taste, sight, and hearing. This book is about your sense of smell.

Your sense of smell helps you to enjoy your food. It also Keeps you safe by giving you warnings about the world around you.

This flower smells nice.

There are smells all around you. What can you smell right now?

Many flowers look pretty and smell nice. What smells do you like?

A dirty dishcloth looks awful and smells bad! What smells don't you like?

Smelly warnings

Smells can give you important warnings. Bad smells warn you when something could harm you.

Smoke has a very strong smell. The smell of smoke can be a warning—something could be on fire! It makes you think of danger.

◀ Firefighters wear masks so they don't breathe in smoke when they are working.

Rotten food smells terrible. This makes you not want to eat it!

What other smells can you think of that give us warnings?

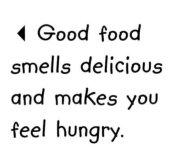

YUM! Smells good!

◀ Good food smells delicious and makes you feel hungry.

A good sniff!

The holes in your **nose** are called **nostrils**. When you **sniff** deeply, smells in the air travel up your nostrils.

What can you smell?

Tiny hairs at the back of your nose detect the smells. This sends a message to your brain. Your brain tells you what you are smelling.

Dogs have a much stronger sense of smell than you. They can smell things that you cannot.

Sniffer dogs help the police to find things and people.

Activity

Try to be a sniffer dog! Put some smelly cheese or a chopped onion on a plate. Ask a friend to hide it.

Can you find the cheese or onion by sniffing it out?

Blocked nose

When you have a cold, your nose gets blocked up and you can't smell very well.

If you have a blocked nose, there can be soft, gooey stuff inside called **mucus**.

◀ Sometimes blowing your nose can help to clear the mucus!

If you have a cold, you may not be able to smell food very strongly. Smell and **taste** work together, so this may mean you do not feel very hungry.

Activity

Make a list of things you often smell. Which smells would you miss if you had a blocked nose? Tick each box:

	Would miss	Wouldn't miss
Fish and chips	✔	
Toothpaste		✔
Soap	✔	
Dirty socks		✔
Chocolate	✔	
Garlic		✔

What's that smell?

If you have smelled something before, your brain remembers it.

The first time you smell a new smell, it seems strong. You have to try to work out what the new smell is. When you smell it again later, you remember it.

You brain also remembers if the smell comes from something good or bad.

I know that smell...

Activity

It's harder to recognize a smell when you can't see what it is coming from.

Put some banana, lemon, chocolate, soap, toothpaste, and dishwashing liquid in six paper cups. Cover the cups with squares of card punched with small holes. Mix the cups by moving them around, then sniff the lids.

Which smells can you detect?

Clean and dirty

You can smell if something is clean or dirty. What would you smell like if you didn't wash for a week?

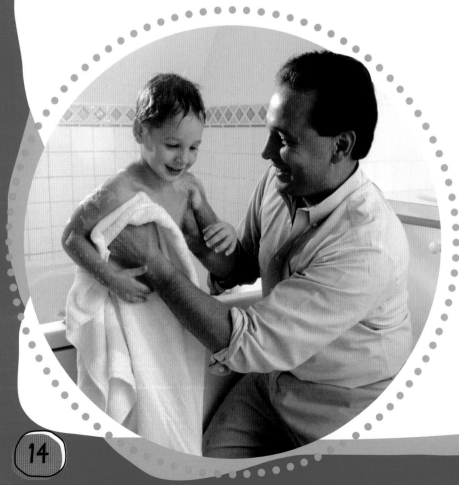

▲ When you do a lot of running or playing, you can get very dirty.

You smell clean when you have had a bath and washed your hair.

14

Dirt with a bad smell is often full of **germs** that can make you ill.

What can you do to keep your home clean and smelling fresh?

▲ Cleaning makes things smell fresh and helps to get rid of germs.

◀ Bag up smelly garbage and put it in the garbage can. Make sure you tie it tightly. Animals have a good sense of smell and may try to get in!

Outdoor smells

Smells are different in the countryside, by the sea, and in the cit

You can tell where you are just by sniffing.

I can smell hay and sheep.

I can smell seaweed.

There are lots of smells in a city. Some can be delicious, and some can be bad!

I can smell traffic fumes and hot dogs.

What else might you smell in the countryside, the seaside, and a city?

Indoor smells

The air inside your home is full of smells. What are the strongest smells in your home?

There are different smells in every room.

▲ What can you smell cooking in your kitchen?

◀ Can you smell toothpaste and soap in the bathroom?

Activity

Can you tell which room you are in just by the smell?

Stand somewhere in your home. Shut your eyes and ask someone to turn you around and around, so you don't know where you are.

Ask them to lead you into different rooms. Give a good sniff. Does the smell tell you which room you are in?

Animals and smell

Animals use their sense of smell to find food and to tell a friend from an enemy.

◀ A mother deer can smell her own baby in a big herd.

▶ A shark sniffs blood in the water and swims toward it to find food.

◀ A cat sniffs its food carefully before it eats, to make sure it is not bad.

20

Flowers smell good to attract insects and birds to drink their nectar. You can use flowers to make **potpourri**. It will make your room smell lovely!

- Collect petals of flowers with a pleasant smell.

- Collect leaves of herbs such as mint.

- Lay them out on paper to dry for a day or two. Mix them together and put them in a bowl.

Glossary

Germ

A tiny living thing that can make you sick if you swallow it or breathe it in. A germ is too small to see without a microscope.

Mucus

Your nose can be full of soft, gooey stuff called mucus or snot which makes it hard to breathe.

Nose

Your nose is the part of your body that you smell with.

Nostrils

The two holes in your nose are called nostrils. Air goes into your nostrils when you breathe and sniff.

Potpourri

A mixture of sweet-smelling petals and leaves.

Rotten

Rotten food has gotten old and gone bad. It is not safe to eat.

Sniff

When you sniff, you breathe deeply. You sniff when you want to smell something.

Sniffer dog

A sniffer dog is trained to use its strong sense of smell to find things.

Taste

The flavor of something in your mouth.

Index

NEXT STEPS

❁ Talk about smelling things safely. Smoke and gases can be poisonous. Remind the children not to spray anything up their nose and that powders such as talc or pepper could damage their nose.

❁ Ask your child to draw a picture of their smiling face, surrounded by pictures of smells that they like. They can also draw a picture of their frowning face, surrounded by smells they don't like. Talk about why they like some smells and dislike others.

❁ Make a smell collage with the children. Collect drawings of things with smells that are pleasant, delicious, disgusting, or give a warning. Sort out the images and stick them onto four large sheets of paper. Make a collection of words to add to the pictures that describe how they smell.

❁ You can learn new smells. Add pinches of herbs and spices to drops of cold cooking oil (to stop powder going up your nose). Smell and name the different herbs and spices. Which ones can your child match to the containers they came from?

❁ Collect pictures of animals with different-shaped noses. Look for their nostrils. Discuss why they might be different, and how they use their noses to breathe and smell.

❁ Ask children to shut their eyes and smell different foods, such as chocolate, orange, cheese, and honey. Can they tell what the food is just by the smell? Afterwards they can eat the food to see if they got it right!